# I'm worried

HODDER
*Wayland*

an imprint of Hodder Children's Books

## Your Feelings

I'm lonely
I'm worried
It's not fair
I'm shy

I'm happy
I feel bullied
I'm special

First published in 1997 by
Wayland Publishers Ltd

Reprinted in 2001, 2002 and 2003 by Hodder Wayland,
an imprint of Hodder Children's Books

Hodder Children's Books,
a division of Hodder Headline Limited,
338 Euston Road, London NW1 3BH
© Hodder Wayland 1997

**Designer:** Jean Wheeler

**British Library Cataloguing in Publication Data**
Moses, Brian, 1950-
I'm worried. - (Your feelings)
1.Worry - Juvenile literature 2.Anxiety - Juvenile literature
I. Title II.Gordon, Mike 1948-
155.4'12'46

ISBN 0-7502-2131-3

Typeset by Jean Wheeler
Printed and bound in Italy by G. Canale & C.S.p.A., Turin

# I'm worried

Written by Brian Moses

Illustrated by Mike Gordon

HODDER
Wayland

an imprint of Hodder Children's Books

When I'm worried
I feel like...

a dog that can't
find his bone...

a balloon that's
losing its air...

a bird that
knows there's
a cat about
somewhere.

5

When I'm worried...

there's a black cloud over my head...

there are butterflies in my tummy...

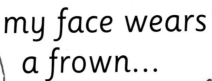

my face wears a frown...

I can't concentrate on my work at school.

When my friends leave me out
of their games and I don't know
what it is that I've done,
I feel worried.

But I soon find
someone else to play with.

When I have to read my poem out at a special assembly and everyone is looking at me, I feel worried.

But once I start reading
I begin to enjoy myself.

When I'm told I'll have to stay in hospital for a night, I feel worried.

But Mum says that she'll
be there holding my hand.

When I know that I'm taking
a test at my swimming club,
I feel worried.

But everyone cheers as
I swim past, and I forget
how worried I was.

When my rabbit is unwell
and leaves the food that
I give him, I feel worried.

But the vet says, 'Don't worry, he'll be all right in a day or two.'

Sometimes adults say...

'Stop worrying, snap out of it.'

'You're a big girl now,
be brave, there's
nothing
to worry
about.'

But adults have their own worries too...

'Is there enough money to pay all the bills?'

Sometimes things that I do
might worry other people...

when I walk along
a high wall...

when I don't look properly
as I cross the road.

When I find myself feeling worried it helps if I think about something pleasant...

a trip to the cinema...

a game with Dad...

playing on
the computer.

It helps if I can talk to
someone about
my worries...

even if it's only little
Ben from next door.

But often worries can disappear
as quickly as they came, just
like the bubbles that float
away on the breeze.

Look up,
not down.
Smile,
don't frown.

# Notes for parents and teachers

Read the book with children either individually or in groups. Ask them how they feel when they are worried. Which of the ideas on pages 4–5 is closest to how they feel, or do they picture themselves in a different way? Ask them to illustrate how they feel.

Talk about the times when children have felt worried. What was the occasion and the outcome? Some of the things that children remember might be used as a basis for a story about worrying. The story could have three parts: (a) the reason for worrying; (b) the event that caused the worry; (c) the aftermath of the event.

Alternatively children may enjoy writing 'list poems' that focus on their own worries:
>  I worry about my ballet exams. Will I do as well
>    as I should?
>  I worry about my spellings. Will I get them right?
>  I worry about… etc.

The poems could also take into account other people's worries:
>  My Dad worries about his garden. Will the slugs eat
>    his cabbages this year?
>  My teacher worries about her class. Will they learn
>    as much as they should?

Some of the book deals with ways in which children cope with worrying. Talk about the ways in which we can overcome our worries. Have children any strategies that they find useful for dealing with worry? What can be done to remove the source of a worry?

Some children might like to act out worrying situations. Other children can suggest ways in which these worries can be reduced.

Can children think of other words which describe how worried we can be – 'nervous', 'anxious', 'tense', 'stressed', 'uneasy', 'fretful', 'agitated', 'distressed', 'dismayed'.

Talk about the phrase, 'the cares of the world'. What does this mean? What are the world's worries? Talk about worries such as pollution, war, crime, homelessness. Can anything be done to reduce these worries?

Through the sharing of picture books such as those mentioned on page 32, talk to children about their worries and reassure them that it is natural to worry and that everyone worries from time to time.

These ideas will satisfy a number of attainment targets in the National Curriculum Guidelines for English at Key Stage 1.

# Books to read

*A Present for Paul* written by Bernard Ashley, illustrated by David Mitchell (Collins Picture Lions, 1996). Pleasure loses sight of her Dad as she helps him with the shopping at the busy market. She is very worried as she tries to find him again.

*A Big Day for Little Jack* by Inga Moore (Walker Books, 1995). When Little Jack Rabbit receives his first party invitation, he is very worried about going on his own. Eventually he overcomes his fears and has a great time. A reassuring read.

*Not a Worry in the World* by Marcia Williams (Walker Books, 1990). Alfie worries about everything until one day he discovers the secret of worries. Then he finds out that he hasn't a worry in the world.

*Moving* written by Michael Rosen, illustrated by Sophy Williams (Puffin, 1995). Moving house is a worrying time for everyone, but particularly if you are the family cat.